The Most Important Story in the World

Words by Maxine McDonald
Pictures by A. K. Newman

UPGlobal / Orlando

This book is available for fundraisers and special promotions.
For more information, or to connect with the illustrator, contact
the publisher at www.unlikelypublicationsglobal.com.

For
Caleb, Micah, and *David*
as you begin your adventure with God to the end of the world.

~Bibi

To
my dear children,

may this book remind you to keep exploring this grand
creation, searching for the little love letters your Heavenly
Father has placed with purpose for you to discover.

~Papa

Audio Version:

Recorded by children ages 3 months to 18 years.

God wrote a story. We call it the Bible.
It has lots of pages, and so I thought I will
Tell you the story in my words this time,
A much shorter version with pictures and rhyme.
There are pieces of it that I know that you've heard,
But it's all one big **STORY** that starts with God's words.

When the story began, God was already there.
He created the world with great wisdom and care.
He made the whole world from nothing but words:
The sun, moon, and stars, plants, fish, reptiles, and birds.
Everything worked just right, as it should.
All was beautiful, organized, clean, fun, and good.
Then God made two people, one at a time.
(I'm sorry, what he said about them won't rhyme.)

They weren't just good. They were **VERY GOOD**.

God's people in Eden (named Adam and Eve)
Were friends with the animals and lived in peace.
They had no problems, no worries, no sin.
God took them on walks in the garden with him.
The world was so happy, and it was all good
As long as they followed one rule like they should:

DON'T EAT THE FRUIT THAT MAKES YOU KNOW ABOUT GOOD AND BAD.

*(The garden is good, so is all that's inside.
Don't eat this fruit. If you do, you will die.)*

One day Eve met a snake when she went for a walk.
The snake was real smart and even could talk.
He said, "You can have the fruit God said don't eat.
Then you'll be wise. God's just selfish, you see.
It makes you like God, knowing both right and wrong."
So Eve ate, and Adam just went right along.
As soon as they ate it, they felt guilt and shame.
Then God said to Adam and Eve and the snake,

"You brought death to the world when you broke my good rule.
You know what **SIN** is now. It's ugly and cruel.
Snake, starting now you will crawl in the dirt.
Eve, from now on having babies will hurt.
Adam, the ground that grows food will be cursed.
Now do you believe me that sin is the worst?"

Because of that day, we all have sin inside.
We steal, hit, kick, yell, pout, say mean things, and lie.
God wrote this story 'cause sin can be fixed.
Want to know how he does it? Then listen to this…

God made a promise to Adam and Eve:
A solution to sin and the bad things we see.
Someday a Man will stop sin as it spreads.
He'll stomp on that snake with his foot 'til it's dead.

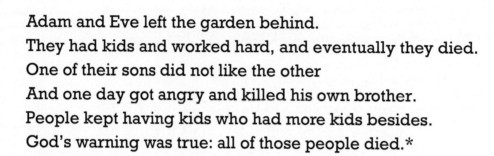

Adam and Eve left the garden behind.
They had kids and worked hard, and eventually they died.
One of their sons did not like the other
And one day got angry and killed his own brother.
People kept having kids who had more kids besides.
God's warning was true: all of those people died.*

Sin spread to everywhere, every which way,
'Til God got so angry and sad that one day
He wiped out the whole world with a **FLOOD**. (But please note:
He kept Noah and some creatures safe in a boat.)

God told them to scatter and fill the whole land.
They thought they came up with a much better plan.
They built a big city and tower so high
They thought it could reach up to God in the sky.
They wanted to settle and stay in one place.
But God wasn't happy that they'd disobeyed.
He scrambled their words so they couldn't keep building.
They couldn't talk to each other, so *mereka*

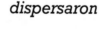

dispersaron

*vezde.***

Now what a ginormous problem we've got!
Everyone's dying and sinning a lot.
They can't talk to each other. The world's gone all wrong.
Can God really fix it? Hang in there! Read on…

*Two people in the Bible never died. Do you know who they are?
Hint: both names start with the letter E.
**they (Indonesian) scattered (Spanish) everywhere (Russian)

God picked a man, and he doesn't say why.
That man wasn't special, big, strong, smart, or wise.
God said to him,

    "Abraham, I promise you
    (And there's nothing at all that you have to do)
    I'll give you a child, and he'll have kids who'll have kids
    And I'll give them a good **LAND** in which they can live.
    I will **BLESS** and protect them for my own name's sake.
    The whole world will be blessed through this **PEOPLE** I make."

We call this promise a big fancy word:

A COVENANT

Because it's important, I want to make sure
That you see that this covenant God made that day
Is how he will take all of our sins away.
Those people whose languages God made a mess
Spread all over the world, and they **ALL** will be blessed.
God's solution to sin can help anyone.
But first we must tell them, and we aren't quite done.
It might not make sense yet, but trust me—it's true—
This covenant should be important to you.

Back to the story: Abraham had a son.
That son was Isaac, who had another one.
Jacob had twelve sons, but one we know best.
Joseph went to Egypt…well, you know the rest.
In Egypt, this people (they're called Israelites)
Had kids who had kids, and time started to fly.
After four hundred years, they were now Egypt's slaves.
It seemed that God's covenant might be too late.
How could slaves be a blessing?
Where would they get a land?
Don't give up just yet! God still had a plan!

God's pretty clever. He got Egypt's king
To train up a leader to set Israel free.
Moses told Pharaoh, "Let my people go!"
But Pharaoh was stubborn and ornery, and so
God sent ten plagues that destroyed all the land.
You think you can count all ten **PLAGUES** on your hands?
Blood, frogs, gnats, and flies, then the animals died.
Boils, hail, and locusts, and darkness outside.
Then God said to Israel, "Put blood on your doors.
I'll kill Egypt's firstborns, but I will spare yours."

Then Pharaoh said, "Go! Please get out of my land!"
God did exactly what he promised Abraham.
He made Israel a **PEOPLE** while they were still slaves.
Remember what else he had promised that day?

A **LAND** and a **BLESSING**.

Then Pharaoh got angry and chased after Moses.
God opened the Red Sea for Israel, then closed it.
He took them to Sinai, the mountain of God,
And on it gave Moses instructions and laws.
He said, "Here's a **COVENANT**, this time with rules.
If you will obey me and don't act like fools,
You'll live in the land that I give you in peace.
Worship just me, and your joy will increase.
I'll bless you, but you must be careful because
Some bad things will happen if you break my laws."
The people said, "We promise we'll do as you say."
God chose priests for his…his…

                    well, there's no other way…

For his **TABERNACLE**…which was a special tent
where Israel worshiped God, and which doesn't
rhyme with anything.

God had delivered them from Pharaoh's hand
And brought them right up to the edge of the land.
He gave clear instructions, and his rules were right.
But Israel didn't trust him to help them to fight.
The people said, "Oh, no! There's soldiers inside!
We'll never win. Let's just run off and hide."
Caleb and Joshua wanted to go.
The people got angry with them and said no.

So God said, "Enough! I promised this land
To Abraham's children. My promise still stands.
But you can't go in it since you won't obey."
Israel was sorry when they heard God say,
"Go back to the desert and die in the sand.
Your children will enter in my promised land."
They wandered the desert for forty long years.
Moses died there, and they mourned him with tears.

Then God said to Joshua, "Time for the fight!
I'm with you. Be brave and keep doing what's right."
Finally, Israel entered the land.
God helped them to conquer with his mighty hand.
They fought with God's enemies and won the day.
The land was now theirs. They built houses and stayed.

It felt good to be home for the wandering tribes.
They followed God's rules until Joshua died.
With Joshua gone, they began to forget.
They worshiped the gods of the people they met.
God said that he was to be worshiped alone.
They bowed down to **IDOLS** of wood, clay, and stone.

It doesn't make sense that they prayed to a rock.
But we aren't much better, and we shouldn't talk.
People do weird things when lost in their sin.
When will God fix it and finally win?

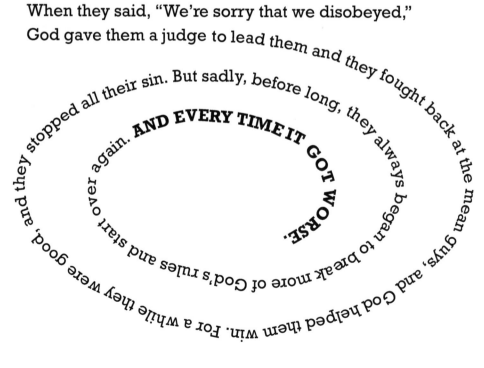

When they disobeyed, God sent some bad guys
Who were mean to the people. They started to cry.
When they said, "We're sorry that we disobeyed,"
God gave them a **JUDGE** to lead them and they
Fought back at the mean guys, and God helped them win.
For a while they were good, and they stopped all their sin.
But sadly, before long, they always began
To break more of God's rules and start over again.

When they disobeyed, God sent some bad guys
Who were mean to the people. They started to cry.
When they said, "We're sorry that we disobeyed,"
God gave them a judge to lead them and they
Fought back at the mean guys, and God helped them win.
For a while they were good, and they stopped all their sin.
But sadly, before long, they always began
To break more of God's rules and start over again.

When they disobeyed, God sent some bad guys
Who were mean to the people. They started to cry.
When they said, "We're sorry that we disobeyed,"
God gave them a judge to lead them and they fought back at the mean guys, and God helped them win. For a while they were good, and they stopped all their sin. But sadly, before long, they always began to break more of God's rules and start over again. **AND EVERY TIME IT GOT WORSE.**

A young woman named Ruth came from way out of town.
She wasn't from Israel, but she lived there now.
She worshiped God. He was pleased with her life.
Ruth then met Boaz and became his wife.
Their great-grandson David would someday be **KING**.
But let's slow back down and not miss anything.

The judges ruled Israel, but things still got worse.
They broke God's covenant Law and were cursed.
"We need a king!" people started to shout.
God was angry when he heard them talking about
How a king would make everything better again.
They forgot that the cause of their trouble was sin.

Saul became Israel's very first king.
At first, he obeyed God, and it even seemed
Like a king was a good thing for Israel to want.
But later Saul sinned, and so God said, "Enough!
I'll choose who Israel's king will now be.
Ruth's great-grandson David will listen to me."
God made a promise to David forever:
Our third—what's that word?—let's say it together:

COVENANT

God said, "One of your sons will rule on your throne.
I'll love him and won't ever leave him alone.
And someday a King from your family again
Will rule Israel forever and ever. Amen."

What could it all mean? Could God promise that now?
Rule forever? But everyone dies. And so how
Could a king come from David and rule on his throne
Without ever dying? Think hard! Do you know?

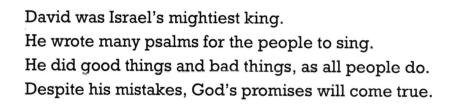

David was Israel's mightiest king.
He wrote many psalms for the people to sing.
He did good things and bad things, as all people do.
Despite his mistakes, God's promises will come true.

Solomon ruled next, just like God had said.
He asked God for wisdom. His kingdom was blessed.
He built a great **TEMPLE**: a big house where priests
Would sacrifice animals like cows and sheep.

Remember that sin always causes a death?
The animals' blood and their last living breath
Was an offering for sin but was never enough
To once and for all just get rid of that stuff.
Sin was always around, always making a mess
In the world God had promised he one day would bless.

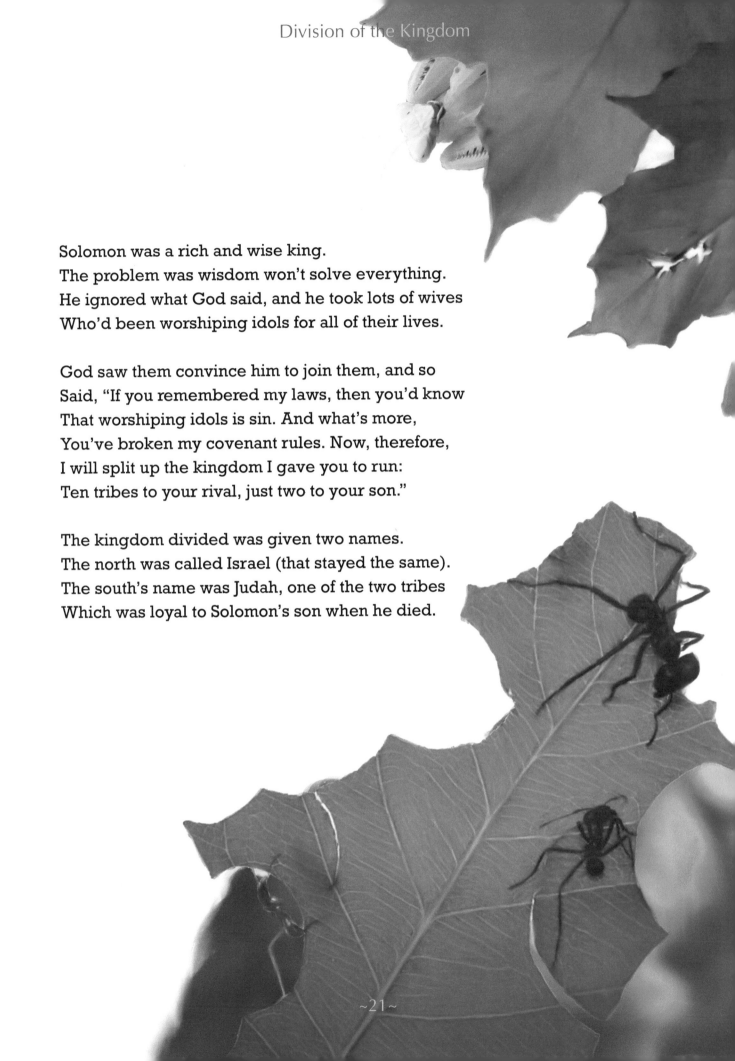

Solomon was a rich and wise king.
The problem was wisdom won't solve everything.
He ignored what God said, and he took lots of wives
Who'd been worshiping idols for all of their lives.

God saw them convince him to join them, and so
Said, "If you remembered my laws, then you'd know
That worshiping idols is sin. And what's more,
You've broken my covenant rules. Now, therefore,
I will split up the kingdom I gave you to run:
Ten tribes to your rival, just two to your son."

The kingdom divided was given two names.
The north was called Israel (that stayed the same).
The south's name was Judah, one of the two tribes
Which was loyal to Solomon's son when he died.

What now? Not only do we still have sin,
Now the kingdom is ruined. What trouble we're in!
Will the promise to David ever come true?
Will a king rule forever? I think so. Do you?

Before it gets better, the story gets worse.
Assyria came and fulfilled God's great curse.
They fought against Israel and took the ten tribes
Away from their land, and lots of them died.
Israel's kings were all evil and bad.
They went into **EXILE** and never came back.

Judah had good kings (not many, but some).
So God waited longer, but judgment did come.
Babylon's armies stole all Judah's land
Because they abandoned God's laws and his plans.
They went into exile just like Israel had,
And things for the kingdom looked **REALLY,**

REALLY

BAD.

If it sounds like God's covenants worked in reverse,
Remember, God promised both blessing and curse.
Now we have no blessing, no king, and no land.
The people are scattered, but God still has plans.
He sent into Israel and Judah a few
Special messengers we call the **PROPHETS** and who
Reminded the people of what God had said.
Their message: "Repent! Obey God or you're dead!"

Joel said, "Watch out for the Day of the Lord!"
Obadiah spoke judgment on Edom's great hordes.
Nineveh's prophet was Jonah, it's true.
But after repenting, their wickedness grew.
Hosea and Amos wrote to Israel,
"You've been unfaithful, but God loves you still."
Isaiah told Judah, "God's wrath is coming!
But then he'll redeem you because he's still loving."

Micah said justice is what pleases God.
Nahum said, "Nineveh, your time is up!"
Habakkuk asked, "Why, God? What hope can you give?"
And then Zephaniah wrote, "Seek God and live."
Said Jeremiah, "Exile will be long."
He wrote Lamentations, a very sad song.
Most kings didn't listen. Most people ignored
What the prophets of God had so faithfully warned.

Ezekiel and Daniel went to Babylon.
In exile, their courage and faith were still strong.
And though things looked bad, God's message was still,

"I'll punish you seventy years. Then I will
Bring all of my people back into the land
And fulfill my covenant with Abraham.
Someday my people will worship me there,
And so will the nations from every which where."

God promised a New **COVENANT** (it's the fourth)
While Israel and Judah were exiled up north.
This new one will not be just like the old Law.
No one will doubt it or break it because
God will write it right onto their hearts, like a book.
It sounds strange, but it's wonderful. Let's take a look:

Judah and Israel will be one again.
God will live with them at last in the end.
So they'll be God's people for once and for all.
And the whole world will know that he is their God.

And did it come true? Did Judah return?
They did! And while they were gone, they had learned
That idols can't save you and God's word comes true.
I'm guessing that's something you already knew.

Zerubbabel built back the temple of God.
Haggai gave them a prophetic prod.
Through Zechariah their hope was revived.
Through Esther in exile God worked in disguise.
Ezra the scribe taught the people the Law.
Then came Nehemiah to build up the wall.
Malachi made sure they stayed on their toes.
But if you read carefully, God's story shows
His presence still did not come back in that day.
His covenants still weren't fulfilled all the way.

What did it mean? Did God just forget?
Never! He can't! He was working, and yet
For four hundred years God stopped writing his book.
It wasn't him dawdling, it's just that it took
That long to prepare all the empires and roads
And the languages, cultures, and legal codes
So God could reveal how the world will be blessed.
It starts with a **BABY**, as you might have guessed.

That baby was **JESUS**, God's very own Son.
He was God. He was Man. And he was the One
Who stomped on the head of that mean, evil snake
When he said he would die on the cross in our place.
He paid for our sin so we don't have to die,
And he rose from the dead and he sits by God's side.

God's promise to David can finally come true
Because Jesus is part of his family, and you
Know that he can be king forever because
He won't sin and won't die. But let's take a pause

And think:
                    If Jesus has come, well, then, why
          Do we still do bad things and sin all the time?
          Did God get it wrong? Has sin actually won?

There's one more big chapter. God's story's not done.

**THE MAIN POINT OF THE BIBLE, THE STORY GOD'S WRITTEN,
THE ONE THING THAT WE SHOULDN'T EVER FORGET
IS THAT ALL OF GOD'S COVENANTS ARE FULFILLED IN JESUS
BUT JESUS HAS NOT FULFILLED ALL OF THEM YET.**

When Jesus went back up to heaven, you see,
He said, "I'll be back. Tell the world about me."
The people who follow him are called the **CHURCH**.
That's us! And together, we can now search
Through the Bible to find out what will happen next.
And we live with hope because we can expect
That someday the waiting and watching will end,
And Jesus will come back from heaven again.

God's plan for the world still isn't quite done.
All peoples are blessed through Jesus, his Son.
But those peoples are scattered, and some still don't know
Sin has a solution. It's our job to go
To everyone everywhere, spread out to search
For places and peoples who don't have a church.

By airplane, by camel, by wooden canoe,
By video, Internet, smartphone apps, too.
By walking, by preaching, by singing, by phone,
By giving, by praying, by sharing their homes.
In writing, in tea rooms, in prisons, in yurts,
In homes built from concrete, bricks, bamboo, and dirt,

God's people are faithfully making hard choices,
To tell God's great story with their hands and voices.

So what is your part in the story God wrote?
Should you jump on a plane or a bike or a boat?
Should you give all your money? Sell all you own?
Learn a new language? Learn how to code?

Maybe! Or maybe there's some other way
For you to be part of God's story today.
That's for you and your parents and God to decide.
I want you to hear it from someone who's tried,
That going with God to the ends of the earth
Is dangerous, scary, and hard, but it's worth
Any price to be part of the story God wrote,
This story of blessings and curses and hope.

REMEMBER: GOD'S PROMISES ALWAYS COME TRUE.

All sad things will end, and the world will be new.
It may seem he's forgotten, might take a long time,
But someday we'll see what he's doing and why.
There will be no more tears and no more goodbyes.
For now, obey God, with one eye on the skies.
We're all in the story God's telling, and when
He's finished, together we'll all shout,

"THE END!"

CPSIA information can be obtained
at www.ICGtesting.com
Printed in the USA
BVHW061017300921
617767BV00004B/351